A Memorial From the City of Milwaukee on the Subject of a Naval Depot, an Armory and an Arsenal

A MEMORIAL

FROM THE

CITY OF MILWAUKEE,

ON THE SUBJECT OF A

Naval Depot, an Armory

AND AN

ARSENAL.

MILWAUKEE

STARR & SON PRINTERS, 212 and 214 EAST WATER STREET

1861.

A MEMORIAL

OF THE CITY OF MILWAUKEE, ON THE SUBJECT OF A NAVAL DEPOT, AN ARMORY AND AN ARSENAL

IN compliance with the resolution of your honorable body, requiring the undersigned to draft a memorial on the subject of an United States Armory, Arsenal and a Navy Depot, we submit the following

MEMORIAL.

That the great North-West, with its 8,000,000 inhabitants, its immense Lake and River Commerce and its Granaries, from which so much of the civilized world is supplied, requires facilities for defence far greater than any now existing, is a proposition hardly requiring an argument.

Whatever may be said of the power of Cotton as influencing the conduct of Foreign Nations towards us, the power of food (which, in times of famine, can be furnished by the North-West alone,) is still greater. The tables of exports from the United States for the last year, show how much of the financial health of our country during the period of Rebellion, has been due to the products of the West. Yet in the whole North-West there is not a single armory, and upon all the great Lakes, but a single armed vessel, and that bearing only one gun. A war with England—an event certainly to be deprecated, but which prudence requires us to prepare for—would drive from the Lakes the immense Commerce, which now not only supplies food to the East, but by bringing back to us the products of their manufactures, gives employment to laborers there The extent of this Commerce may be conjectured from the fact, that from the single Port of Milwaukee, there has been shipped in wheat (and in flour reduced to wheat) nearly 17,000,000 bushels during the past year. The interruption of navigation upon the Lakes would force us either to find an outlet by the way of the Mississippi, if by that time Rebellion shall have been crushed, or to seek the East by routes so indirect and expensive, as almost to exclude the idea of large exportations. Pennsylvania, New York and New England would hardly, from such an event, suffer less than the West It has been well urged, that if at the same time, England and the South should jointly war with us, and while ngland should command Lake Erie with her fleet, the South should push her armies up through Western Virginia and across the Ohio, there might be danger of an entire interruption of communication between the East and the West. This danger is doubtless remote, but even the possibility should be guarded against. Our conclusion then is, that at every cost, the United States should have control over the Lakes. The common impression, that from the mere fact of a vast superiority of our commerce and merchant marine on the Lakes, we could create a navy much sooner than our neighbor, is not altogether sound. Our treaty with England--equal, at the time it was made—has been rendered most unequal by the construction within her own waters of the Welland Canal. While each party is nominally limited by the treaty to one vessel on each Lake, England can by her control over that canal, introduce at once any number of small gun boats. In fact, for practical purposes of naval marine, that canal makes the Lake, to the English navy, a part of the Ocean.

Long before our merchant propellers and steamers could be made available for war purposes, the Lakes would be swarming with English gun boats of small size, but still of draught sufficient for operating upon our waters   It may well be urged that as the treaty was made with reference to waters owned by the United States and England in common, it cannot apply to Lake Michigan, which is wholly within the United States. But even if this should be held otherwise, and if Government should be unwilling to give the six months notice necessary under the treaty, to abrogate that provision, it would still be judicious to have a naval depot at one of the ports of Lake Michigan, at which such means for fitting out a navy might be collected, as would involve the least possible delay, in event of a war. If (as each of us should hope) there should be no war with England, this naval depot would still be useful.

The Welland Canal could be made as available for us in times of peace with England, as to her in time of war. In no part of the country are materials for ship-building more easily procured, or cheaper ; our shipwrights may, in workmanship, well challenge competition ; and Lake navigation, land-locked as it is, requires far more skill, and trains the sailor to far greater vigilance and caution than does navigation on the broad expanse of the ocean.

Gun-boats of light draft, but of the best possible construction, may here be built, and manned with sailors inferior to none in the world; they could then be sent to the ocean ready for immediate service. Connected with the naval depot should be an armory and an arsenal. But as this subject has already received the attention of Government, and the President has favorably mentioned it in his message, any lengthy discussion of it here will be unnecessary.

If Congress should conclude to establish a naval depot, an armory or an arsenal, at any point in the North-West, the next question will be where to locate it.

We hold that such location must be not far from Lake Michigan, for the following reasons:

1st. Because, considered in regard to the whole North-West, it is nearly central.

2d. Because it is wholly within the United States, and its ports are susceptible of defence at small expense, against any attack by water.

3d. Because it is so far remote from the locality of the present Rebellion as to be free from danger from that quarter.

4th. Becouse by means of water communication and the numerous railroads radiating from its various ports, facilities are afforded in a pre-eminent degree for cheap and rapid transportation of arms, ammunition and troops, to all other parts of the North-West.

The location of a Naval Depot has been settled by nature. For that purpose a harbor, which may safely be entered in the most violent storm, and capacious enough to accommodate a nu-

merous fleet, is absolutely necessary; and Milwaukee has the
only harbor on Lake Michigan, answering this description. Here
two rivers, the Milwaukee and Menominee, and the Kinnikinnick
stream conjoin to form a basin, which would accommodate all the
commerce of the Lakes; a broad Bay, protected on the north
and south by points of land extending into the Lake, renders less
difficult the entrance into the harbor in boistering weather. And
one of the two mouths of the harbor itself has been so improved
at the expense of the city, as to be the best on either of the
Lakes.

The Milwaukee River, broad and deep, and protected on each
side of land gradually rising into high bluffs, which break the vio-
lence of the winds, is navigable to the dam : the Menominee, not
so broad, but in other respects equally good, can be navigated for
about one and a half miles : the Kinnikinnick, at its confluence
with the other, near the south mouth of the Harbor, aids in the
formation of the magnificent basin before referred to.

This suggests another advantage possessed by Milwaukee, and
which, while the national wealth is taxed to its utmost to put
down Rebellion, is of no small importance—we refer to the low
price at which suitable grounds can be purchased.

From the extent of our harbor facilities, and of the ground
touched by navigable water, which would enable Milwaukee to accommodate the commerce of all the Lake cities put together, suit
able lands for a Naval Depot may be purchased at a small
cost.

Chicago, fortunate in its larger population and more extended
commerce, but unfortunate in its smaller harbor and in the danger-
ous access to it, already finds its narrow stream taxed to the ut-

most ; it would be safe to affirm that no suitable place for a Naval Depot or an Armory could be purchased there for less than millions, and that such purchase would operate to the serious detriment of its general commerce, now so hardly accommodated.

If it be there proposed to donate grounds on the Lake shore to government, the cost will be even greater, for Government would not only be forced to construct a breakwater, or in other words, manufacture an artificial harbor in order to have access to the grounds, but would yearly be at enormous expense for repairing.

The same argument applies to an Armory , it should be at a point where coal, iron and other materials could be immediately delivered from vessels , great expense in the way of re-handling and transportation would be involved in the fact of any other location.

If a position too remote from the Lake to be in danger from hostile vessels should be desired, the winding Menominee affords such position completely screened by high bluffs from the Lake, but which on nearly every side would be surrounded by navigable water.

WATER - POWER.

The dam across the Milwaukee River at about 2 miles from its mouth, creates a fine water power, which, if desirable, might be made available for mechanical purposes connected with the Armory.

CHEAPNESS OF MATERIALS.

There is no point on the Lakes at which materials necessary either for erecting shops, building ships or manufacturing arms, can be more cheaply procured than at Milwaukee.

MATERIALS FOR BUILDING.

Milwaukee has long been famous for the quality and beauty of her brick; there is no considerable city on the Lakes, which has not been a purchaser of them to some extent; in our exports they have formed no inconsiderable item ; made within the limits of the city, they can be delivered here at any point at a price much lower than that which must be given for brick of like quality at any other port Stone, too, may be easily obtained within three miles from the city, from inexhaustible quarries.

SHIP TIMBER AND LUMBER.

Situate in a country covered with timber of all kinds, easily accessible to vessels from Northern Michigan, and the lumber regions of Wisconsin; with harbor facilities, which render the actual landing of timber here both safe and cheap, Milwaukee can furnish ship-timber and lumber at as low rates as any other place.

CHARCOAL.

For a like reason Charcoal must always be cheaper here than at places south of it. The belt of timber which commencing in the extreme North runs out about 20 miles south of Milwaukee, leaves a prairie or low country beyond, almost destitute of timber.

COAL.

The numerous vessels employed in carrying East from Milwaukee the products of Wisconsin, frequently return in ballast and generally are willing to receive coal at the ports on Lake Erie and bring it here at a price little beyond the cost of loading and unloading it; coal may therefore practicably be had as cheaply

2

here as at Erie, Cleveland and Buffalo, and more cheaply than at any port south of us.

IRON.

Those portions of Wisconsin and Michigan constituting the south shose of Lake Superior, furnish iron equal to any in the world; and that iron can be procured at Milwaukee as cheaply as at any port on Lake Michigan. Iron from the Eastern States can be brought here by water at small cost; the Mayville iron in our own State is but a short distance from Milwaukee, and upon the route of the Milwaukee & La Crosse R. R It will be of the greatest value both because the quantity is great, and because the whole surrounding county is covered with timber, and charcoal to work it can be had there at a very low price.

But pre-eminently over all other cities on the Lakes, Milwaukee can boast of the health of its climate, the skill of its mechanics, the cheapness of living and the consequent cheapness of labor.

In no part of the United States can men live so cheaply, and yet with comfort, as here, comfortable houses can be rented at low prices, and the neighborhood of Milwaukee entirely free from waste marshes, is occupied to a great degree by laborious gardiners, who make our market one of the best and cheapest in the world. We, of course, do not refer to the cereals, because although the advantage in quality in that respect is somewhat in favor of Milwaukee: prices are necessarily about equal at all points on the lake. But we refer to those articles purchased at the market and which form the staple food of the laboring class.

For this reason mechanics of all kinds can afford to work here at much lower rates than in most of our Sister Cities. Out of our population of 50,000 inhabitants, they form an important

portion; and Milwaukee is justly proud of them. We will add
that the first locomotive ever constructed in the West was made
here. The healthfulness of Milwaukee is a matter of too much
notoriety to require extended notice. With ground rising gradually from the water, so as at once to secure convenient business
streets and healthful locations for residences; entirely free from
the neighborhood of those wide marshes, which too frequently in
the West poison the atmosphere; with a system of drainage established by nature, which in the warm months relieves the streets
entirely of those stenches which sometimes render other cities
intolerable; its inhabitants have had an exemption from disease
enjoyed by few on the continent.

Nor is Milwaukee less fortunate in its position, or in the means
of transportation. A glance at the map of the North-West will
show Milwaukee to be nearly central in that group of States ;
and situated on the great Northern route from the Mississippi to
the East, with a harbor from which each day during the cold
months of winter, propellers and steamers have during the past two
years crossed the Lake—she has in that respect advantages not
shared by rivals. By means of the Milwaukee and La Crosse
Railroad, she has the Northern and direct connection with Minnesota ; by means of the Milwaukee and Prairie du Chien with
Iowa ; by means of the Milwaukee, Green Bay and Chicago
Railroad, with Chicago and her system of Railroads, and by
means of other South-Western connections, with Central and
Western Illinois. As water is so much cheaper than land carriage, and as Milwaukee through its position on the Lake and its
harbor, has so great a pre-eminence in water carriage, that alone
should almost determine the question in its favor.

It is hardly necessary to urge economy as well as convenience, as a reason why an Armory, Arsenal and Naval Depot should be united at one place ; this is too apparent to require comment, and we have accordingly treated the whole as one proposition.

It may be proper in conclusion, without impeaching the justice of the intentions of Congress, to call their attention to the man_ ner in which Wisconsin has been treated by the general government. Hers has rather been the share of a step-child, than of a legitimate child of the Union. Charleston, Savannah, Mobile and various other places on the Eastern and Southern coast, less than Milwaukee in population, and far less important in commerce, have never asked appropriations for harbor improvements or defences, without a favorable response from Congress ; even most of the harbors in other States on the Lakes, have been improved or constructed by Congress

But the Lake ports of Wisconsin have been compelled, out of their own means, (which in young cities just struggling into commercial importance, are naturally limited,) to improve their own harbors, The harbor at Chicago, from the mere fact of being almost the extreme South port, is necessarily local in its use; yet it has been constructed at the expense of the government, the harbor of Milwaukee, from its position and capacity may be a place of refuge in a storm to all vessels on the Lake ; it adds to the safety of the commerce of all the bordering States—in other words, in its usefulness it is not merely local but national; yet Milwaukee was compelled out of its own treasury, and at an expense of over $260,000, to improve their harbor.

Of all the States included within the Virginian grant, and whose rights of admission were defined by the Ordinance of

1787, Wisconsin was the youngest. The difficulties between Ohio, Michigan, Indiana and Illinois, on the subject of boundaries, were all settled and compensated by spoliation of Wisconsin.

Galena, and even Chicago itself, would have belonged to Wisconsin, but for compensation to Illinois ; and geography is outraged by Michigan's crossing the Lake and taking a portion of the shore of Lake Superior (having no interest in common with it) as compensation for a difference between it and Ohio

When Wisconsin was a Territory under the guardianship of Congress, a grant was made to aid in the construction of a canal from Milwaukee to Rock River—but as was to have been expected from the half grown legislation of that period—the grant was chiefly wasted, and no canal was built ; yet by the act admitting Wisconsin into the Union, and by the construction of the department, that grant was charged to the new State as so much received by it and to be accounted for by it ; or in other words, the guardian charges the ward when of age, the waste by unthrift occasioned by the guardian himself

Of the other grants made by Congress to the State, little favorable can be said. The North-Eastern, procured by Chicago and Illinois influence, belongs to the Chicago and North-Western Railroad Co ; and if of little value in itself, it has facilitated the construction of a road to give to Chicago that commerce and to Illinois that wealth, which otherwise would have been retained in Wisconsin ; the title to the lands included in the North-Western land grant, has, under influences hostile to the commerce of Wisconsin, been retained by the general government, and the Milwaukee and La Crosse Road has been built without receiving any portion of the grant. The only remaining grant to Wisconsin was to aid the construction of the Fox River and Wisconsin Canal. If that has been of some benefit to the State, the grant was nevertheless loaded with such conditions, that while it in fact took no dollar from the treasury of the United States, it withdrew from market and settlement large tracts of country, and has failed to accomplish for the State much that was expected from it. The above comprises the list of special favors from the General Government to Wisconsin.

In alluding to Chicago, we have been influenced by the fact that she is the only competitor on the Lake, and some comparison was necessary. Milwaukee has shown none of those feelings of jealousy and hostility so often manifested by her great and older Commercial Rival. Content with a growth in commerce, in population, and in wealth, that has kept pace with the growth of Wisconsin, Minnesota and Northern Iowa, Milwaukee has regarded with pride, as a North-Western city, the wonderful progress of Chicago, and has witnessed with admiration the united effect of government patronage and individual enterprise in overcoming natural difficulties, and in building up over places more fortunately situated, a great city. The touch of Government there has in creative power, rivalled Aladdin's Lamp, and out of the waste produced palaces, population, commerce, wealth. But this result is due as much to the enterprise of her people, their united action on all questions affecting her, and their constant and jealous watchfulness over all her interests, as to the action of government as represented by her harbor, by the Canal connecting Chicago and Illinois River, by the Illinois Central R. R., and by that uniform government policy (inducted by Douglas and other representatives of the local interests of Illinois) constantly favoring her growth. But we insist that all parts of the

Union are equally entitled to the protection and favor of government, and that we may well refer in a question of this kind (where the advantages of location on our side are at least equal,) to the benefits bestowed on other States and Cities, and the coldness with which we have been treated. If we were not conscious that the great objects of an Armory, an Arsenal and a Naval Depot, would be advanced by a location in Milwaukee, we would not urge this argument. We made no claim to a Marine Hospital (now established at Chicago,) because the greatest commercial city presented advantages for such an institution.

But under the policy of Congress, Armories and Naval Depots should not necessarily be located in the greatest cities, as evidenced by Watervleit, Springfield and Harper's Ferry as to Armories, and by Charleston, Brooklyn and Norfolk as to Naval Depots. A city like Milwaukee, with 50,000 inhabitants, with skilful mechanics, where living and labor are cheap and materials easily procured, is large enough for such purposes.

And we claim that under these circumstances we may fairly point to past legislation in order to show that we are in justice now entitled to some consideration.

JAMES S BROWN,
HARRISON LUDINGTON,
NELSON WEBSTER,
J. C. U. NIEDERMANN.

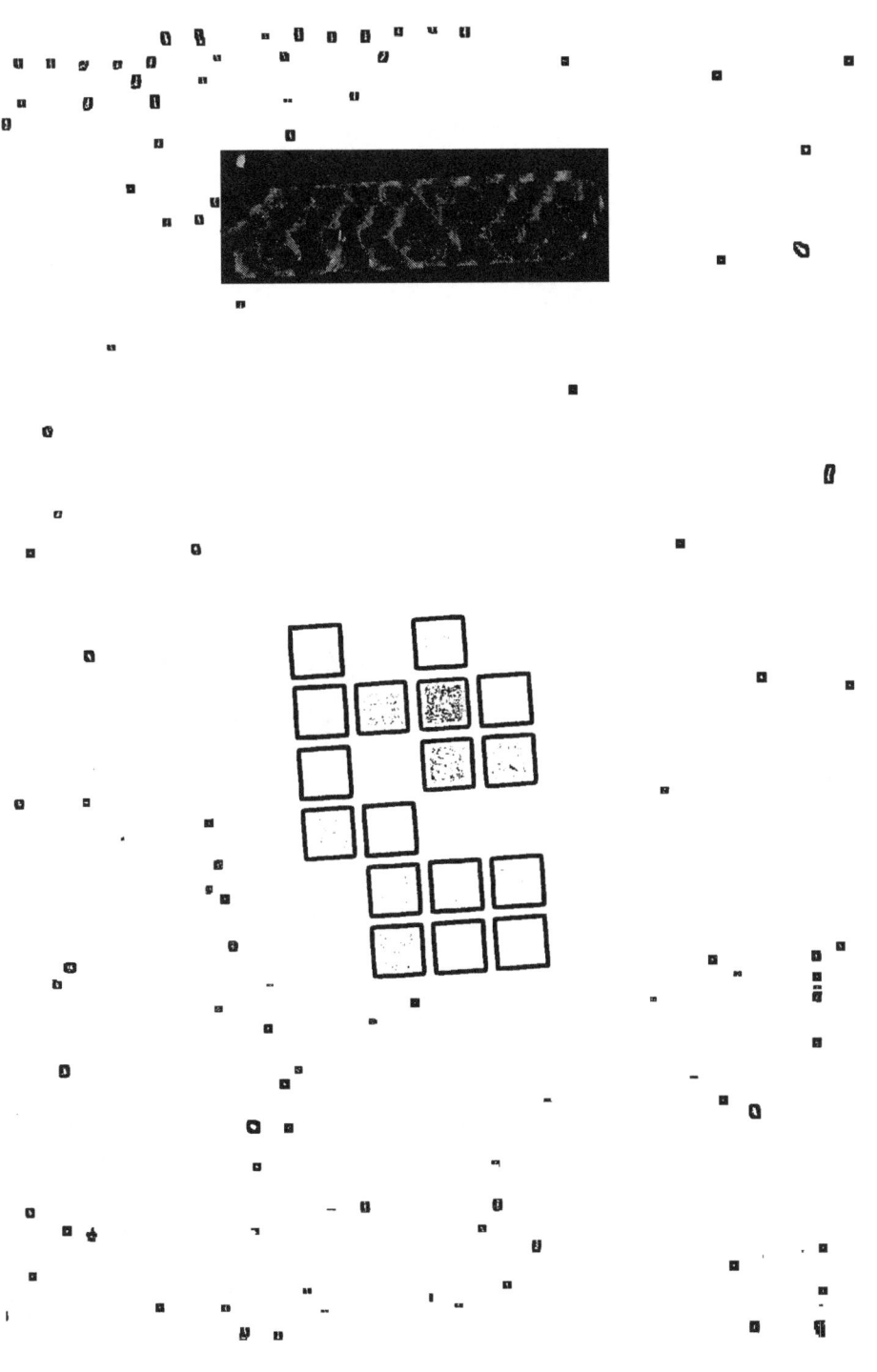

CPSIA information can be obtained
at www.ICGtesting.com
Printed in the USA
BVHW04*1032310718
523166BV00008B/110/P